Following a Star

KEVIN MAYHEW LTD
Rattlesden Bury St Edmunds
Suffolk England
IP30 0SZ

ISBN 0 86209 564 6
Catalogue No. 1108126

Printed in Great Britain

Following a Star

Retold from Scripture by Margaret Joy
and illustrated by Arthur Baker

Kevin Mayhew

Long ago, before people knew about electricity, there were no torches or street lamps to lighten the darkness. So the moon was very important because, when it shone, the night didn't seem quite so dark.

The stars were important, too. They were like signposts in the sky. Sailors and other travellers could find their way by looking at the stars.

Some men – astronomers – spent their lives studying the stars; they knew how important stars were to people on earth.

About two thousand years ago, a new star appeared in the sky. Some astronomers noticed it and were puzzled.

'It's moving across the sky towards the west,' said Caspar.

'I think it has a message for the people on earth', said Balthasar.

'Yes,' said Melchior, 'I think it means that a new king has been born – the most important king ever born on earth.'

'Well, why don't we follow the star and find him?' said Caspar.

'Why not?' they all said, as they shook hands solemnly. What a journey this would be!

So they prepared to set out to follow the star.

'We must take plenty of money,' said Caspar, 'this journey might take months.'

'And we'll need many camels and horses,' said Melchior, 'to carry us and all our belongings.'

'And we must take rich gifts,' said Balthasar, 'to honour this great new king. Let's give him gold, for he's a king; and frankincense, for one from God, and myrrh – that's good for soothing wounds.'
'And for rubbing on a baby's gums when teeth are coming through,' said Melchior.

At last they set off. For days and weeks the star led the way. They crossed deserts and mountains. They rode through rivers, fields and forests. They met bandits and fierce animals, and many other dangers.

It was burning hot by day, and freezing at night. But still the star led them onwards, shining as brightly as ever.

'We've been travelling for weeks,' sighed Caspar, 'surely the star will stop somewhere soon.'

At last they reached the great city of Jerusalem.

Balthasar shaded his eyes. 'I can see a palace!' he cried, 'Perhaps that's where the star is leading us.'

Messengers rode out to meet them.

'This is the palace of King Herod,' they said. 'He likes to meet any strangers who travel past here. Let us take you to him.'

In the great hall of the palace a herald announced them.

'Your Majesty, these travellers are wise men from far in the east. They have been following a star which rose in the heavens. They think it will lead them to a baby who will be a great new king, the greatest king there has ever been on earth.'

King Herod was furious and very worried. *He* was the king, and no one else!

But he hid his feelings, and said to the wise men: 'Please stay, and refresh yourselves after your long and dangerous journey.'

King Herod secretly invited all the important men of Jerusalem to the palace.

'You're the brainy ones around here,' he snapped, 'you're supposed to be advising me! What have you been doing all this time? What's this I hear about a baby who is going to be the greatest king in all the world? Where's he going to be born? For heaven's sake, tell me!'

The chief priests and teachers bowed. 'He is going to be born in Bethlehem, your Majesty,' they said, 'the village down the road, not far from here.'

By now it was nearly nightfall. The wise men from the east were eager to set off again.

'Farewell!' said King Herod, putting on a false smile. 'When you find the child, make sure you let me know exactly where he is. I, too, would like to visit him.'

The wise men agreed, and set off towards Bethlehem.

The star they had been following appeared in front of them again, and they were overjoyed.

Then, suddenly, it stopped.

The wise men looked at one another. Had they reached the end of their journey at last?

'Its light is shining down on the house over there,' whispered Caspar.

'Let's go and see,' said Balthasar and Melchior very quietly.

They knocked on the door, and a man came to open it.

'We've travelled for weeks, following a star, to see a special baby,' said Caspar. 'Is he here?'

A woman's voice came from inside, 'Who is it, Joseph?'

'It's some travellers, Mary,' the man replied. 'They've come a long way to see Jesus.'

'Ask them in,' said the woman's voice.

The wise men went inside.

The light of the star seemed to fill the whole room.

But the wise men only had eyes for the little child, Jesus, who was there with his mother.

They felt happier than they had ever felt before in their lives.

The time just slipped past.

But at last they had to go.

They laid down their gifts, and left.

That night Caspar dreamt that an angel came to him, warning them not to go back to King Herod.

'That's funny, I had the same dream,' said Balthasar in the morning. 'So did I!' said Melchior.

'We'd better go back to the east by a different way,' said Caspar.

'Agreed!' said the other two. 'That King Herod is a nasty piece of work! It would be dreadful if we caused any harm to come to little Jesus.'

So the wise men returned home by a different road.

Joseph, too, had a dream.

An angel appeared to him,
sent by God, and said, 'King Herod
is looking for little Jesus. He
wants to kill him. You must take
the baby and his mother, and
escape to Egypt.'

'We are in God's hands,' said
Joseph. He got up, took the child
and his mother, and set off for
Egypt, where King Herod wouldn't
be able to find them.

When King Herod found out that the visitors from the east had tricked him, he was furious.

But Jesus, Mary and Joseph had already escaped; they were safe.

And the wise men were far away, joyfully praising God on their journey home to the east.

Note for parents:
This story can be found in the Gospel of Matthew, chapter 2, verses 1-16.